Hi, I am
SALLY
SLICE

Hi, I am
TOMMY
TOPPER

The A-Z of Junior Golf

by
Dean Davis
Professional Golfer

First edition published in Great Britain 2003 by Dean Davis
Second edition published in Great Britain 2014 by Dean Davis

Illustrations by Flaming Pumpkin Ltd
www.flamingpumpkin.co.uk
Design by Dean Davis

ISBN 9780954466503

Printed and bound in Great Britain
by Printondemand-worldwide

Meet our junior golfers...

Hi, I am

HARRY
HOOK

Hi, I am
SUZY
STRAIGHT

A is for Ace

Ace

An ace is a hole in one. Tommy hits his ball from the tee into the hole and scores an ace.

and Aim

Aim

Harry aims the club at the hole.

B is for Bunker,

Buggy, Ball, Birdie **and** Bogey

Bunker

Harry has hit his ball into a bunker. The bunker has sand in it. Try not to go into a bunker when you are playing golf.

Buggy

Sally and Suzy are riding in the buggy. They can play golf faster if they ride in a buggy.

Ball

The ball is round and can come in different colours.

Birdie

Tommy has just had a birdie. The hole usually takes 3 shots, but Tommy played it in 2 shots – one under par. That's a birdie!

Bogey

Suzy has just had a bogey. The hole usually takes 3 shots, but Suzy played it in 4 - one over par. That's a bogey!

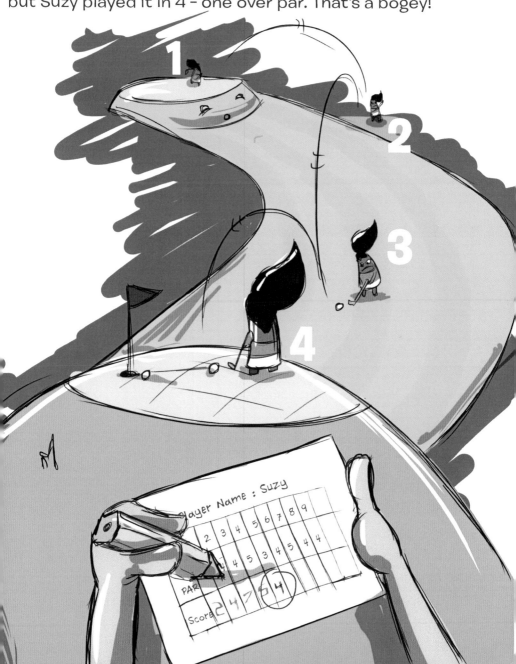

C is for Carry,

Carry

Tommy and Sally like
to carry their clubs.

Clothing and Clubs

Clothing

You need to wear the correct clothing when you play golf. Most golf clubs expect you to wear shirts with collars, trousers, shorts or skirts. T-shirts and jeans are not acceptable. Tommy and Sally are wearing suitable clothing, but Harry is not.

Clubs

You use a golf club to hit the ball. Some shots need different clubs. You are only allowed a maximum of 14 clubs in your golf bag when you play a round of golf.

D is for Driver, Divot

Driver

Harry has got a new driver. You use this club when you want to hit the ball a long way from the tee.

Divot

When you hit a shot you can sometimes make a divot. A divot is a piece of turf dug out of a grass surface with a golf club when you hit the shot. Always replace your divot.

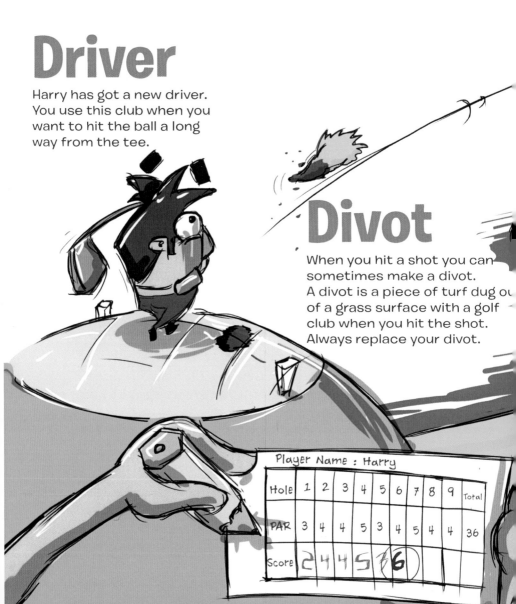

Player Name : Harry

Hole	1	2	3	4	5	6	7	8	9	Total
PAR	3	4	4	5	3	4	5	4	4	36
Score	2	4	4	5	6	6				

Dog Leg and Double Bogey

Dog Leg

At this hole, the shape of the fairway has a bend in it - it looks like a dog's back leg.

Double Bogey

Harry has just had a double bogey. The hole usually takes 4 shots, but Harry played it in 6 - TWO over par. That's a double bogey!

E is for
Electric Trolley,

Electric Trolley

Tommy does not like carrying his clubs. He has an electric trolley to carry his clubs for him.

Eighteen

Eighteen holes make a full game of golf. The last hole is called the eighteenth hole.

Eagle **and** Eighteen

Eagle

The hole Harry is playing is a par 5. Harry played it in 3 shots - that's an eagle! TWO under par, it's even better than a birdie!

Player Name : Harry

Hole	10	11	12	13	14	15	16	17	18	Total
PAR	3	4	4	5	3	4	5	3	5	72
SCORE	2	5	7	6	3	6	5	4	(3)	

F is for Four, FORE!

Four

You can only have a maximum of four people playing in a group at one time.

FORE!

Sally shouts FORE because she has hit her ball and can see someone in the way. She shouts FORE to warn the player to move out of the way.

Flagstick **and** Fairway

Flagstick

The flagstick shows you where the hole is. The flagstick must be taken out when you are on the green playing your shot. When you finish playing the hole you must put the flag back in the hole.

Fairway

The area between the tee box and the putting green where the grass is cut even and short is called the fairway. It is the best place to hit your shot. If your ball goes off the fairway, it may be hard to play your next shot.

G is for Green

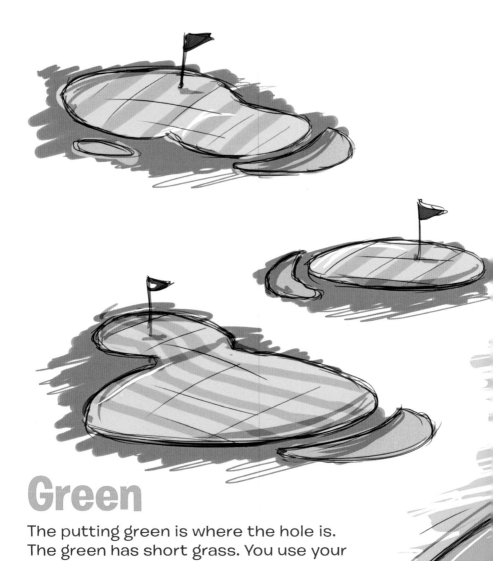

Green

The putting green is where the hole is.
The green has short grass. You use your
putter on the green.

and Good Golfing

Good Golfing

Follow the rules of golf like Suzy, Tommy, Sally and Harry.

H is for Hazard,

Hazard

A hazard is a trap to catch you. It can be a bunker or water. It's hard to get out of a hazard.

Hook

Harry has just hooked his ball - his shot has curved sideways to the left. (If Harry was left-handed, his hook would go right.)

Hook, Hole **and** Hands

Hole

There are eighteen holes on a golf course. Each one has a small hole with a flag in it. The aim of the game is to get your ball to drop into the hole on the green.

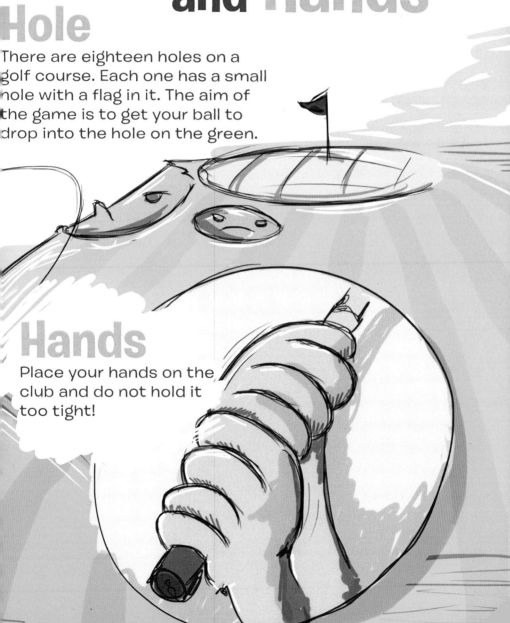

Hands

Place your hands on the club and do not hold it too tight!

I is for Instructor

If you want to improve your golf, you need some lessons. An instructor (sometimes called a coach or teacher) will help you to play better golf.

J is for Juniors

Juniors are young people who play golf. You are the golf stars of the future!

L is for Long

Suzy hits her ball with her driver and she hits it a long way.

M is for Metal and Medal

Metal

The head of the end of the golf club is made from metal.

Medal

Suzy wins her first competition and gets a medal.

N is for Nine Holes

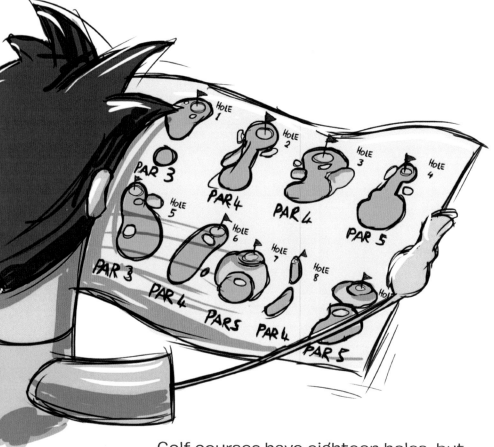

Golf courses have eighteen holes, but you can choose to play nine of them for a shorter round.

The holes are different lengths: small holes are par 3, longer holes are par 4 and the longest are par 5. You always start from Hole 1.

O is for
Out Of Bounds

Out of bounds is marked by
white posts.

Harry has hooked his ball to
the left, it has gone beyond
the white posts and is
out of bounds.

P is for Pitching, Par,

Pitching

Pitching is when you play a short shot using a pitching wedge onto the green.

Par

The number of shots you are meant to play from the tee to the hole is called par. If you do it in fewer, it is under par.

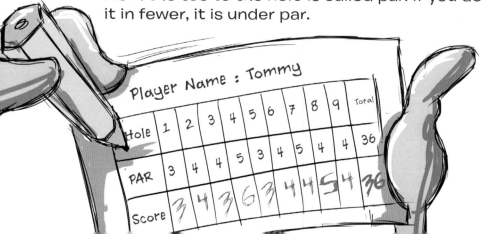

Player Name : Tommy

Hole	1	2	3	4	5	6	7	8	9	Total
PAR	3	4	4	5	3	4	5	4	4	36
Score	3	4	3	6	3	4	4	5	4	36

Pitchfork **and** Putt

Pitchfork

Do not forget your pitchfork to repair your pitch mark or dent on the green.

Putt

Tommy is on the putting green. He uses his putter to play this shot and putt the ball into the hole.

Q is for Quiet

You must be quiet when other people are playing or you may put them off their shot.

R is for Rules and Rough

Rules

You must know the rules when you play golf. Sally is reading her rule book.

Rough

Rough is the thick grass on the side of the fairway. It's much harder to play from long grass. Try to keep your ball on the fairway and out of the rough.

S is for Swing, Shoes, Spikes

Swing

A golf swing is when you lift the club back over your head and then swing the club through to the ball. Harry has got his swing just right.

Shoes and Spikes

Golf shoes have spikes to give you grip when playing. Tommy has just slipped over because he is not wearing proper golf shoes. Harry is safe because he is wearing his golf shoes.

Slice and Shot

Slice

Sally has just sliced her ball – her shot has curved sideways to the right. (If Sally was left-handed, her slice would go left.)

Shot

You play a shot every time you hit the ball. Suzy always hits straight down the fairway.

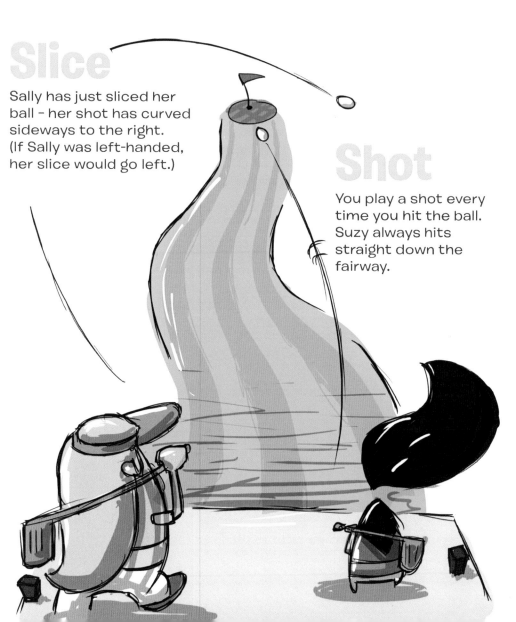

T is for Teeing Ground, Tees and Top

Teeing Ground

When you start your game of golf you have to tee the ball on the teeing ground. There are different areas on the tee, which are marked with white, yellow and red markers. White tees are for competitions, yellow tees are for men and red tees are for ladies and juniors.

Tees

Tees are different sizes and different colours. At each hole Suzy puts her ball on a tee peg for her first shot. She has to find the right tee to use.

Top

Tommy has topped his ball. He hit it on the top and it has just rolled away.

U is for Umbrella

It's raining, so Harry is putting up his umbrella. If it looks like rain, take an umbrella so you don't get wet.

V is for Visor

When the sun is strong, look after your eyes. Wear a visor or a peaked cap. You should drink lots of water, too.

W is for Water

Harry has hit his ball into the water. Don't go after your ball if it goes in the water - it may be deep. Harry will have an extra shot added to his score for hitting his ball into the water.

NO SWIMMING

X is for eXercise

Exercise before you play
so you do not hurt yourself
when you play golf.

Y is for Yardage

You will see markers on the course that tell you how many yards it is to the hole. (In some countries they use metres for distance.)

Z is for Zig Zag

Harry is zigzagging down the fairway, instead of playing straight. He needs to have a lesson to improve his golf.

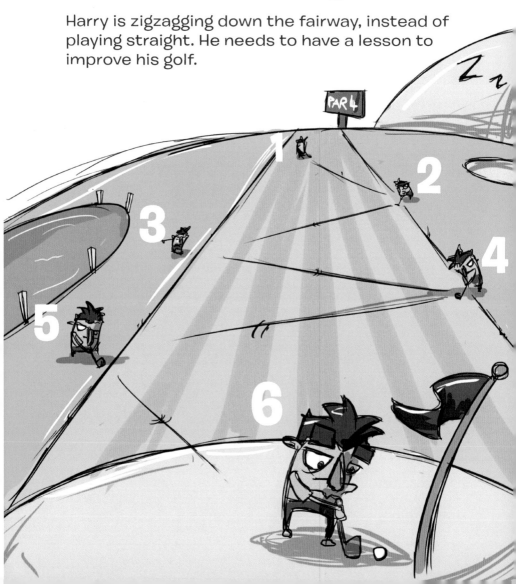

We hope you've enjoyed reading our
A-Z of Junior Golf.

Goodbye from
Sally, Harry, Suzy and Tommy.

We hope to see you again soon.

Getting Started

What is the best way to begin playing golf?

Most golf clubs and golf courses will have a teaching professional and it is best to have a few lessons before you pick up any bad habits. This way you can learn the basics and build the confidence to go out and play.

Most golf clubs will be able to supply equipment so you or your parents do not have to purchase any golf clubs until you are ready.

It is best to find a golf club that is actively encouraging juniors to play golf and has a driving range and practice facilities. Some courses now have a 9-hole Academy Course which is a great way to begin playing the game, whilst some will have a junior organiser who will organise events for all the juniors of the club. This is also a great way for you to meet new friends.

Clubs

When you start playing golf it is important that you have golf clubs that are the right size for you. With the right choice of clubs, you will learn a really good swing and have lots of fun.

Avoid clubs that are far too big for you and adult clubs that have been cut down.

To hit great shots, to get the ball flying high and to enjoy your golf, we recommend you take a look at the range of clubs available from Golphinforkids.

Golf professionals recommend these clubs to all kids because there are so many advantages

- They are much lighter
- The club heads are larger than normal traditional clubs
- They are suitable for boys and girls of all ages
- They come in a range of colours

Using these clubs will help to make golf easier to learn and much more fun - after all golf is all about having fun!

What Is Golf Etiquette?

People who do not play golf might tell you that golf is all about stuffy old-fashioned rules - WRONG!

Golf Etiquette is simply a guide on how to behave on a golf course. When you start to play golf it is important that you play safely and sensibly and think about other golfers. The golf clubs and golf balls you use can easily cause a serious injury if someone is hit or they are used incorrectly.

Here are some guides to golf etiquette:

- Avoid slow play

- Keep your game moving

- Only hit a ball if it is safe to do so and when the group in front is out of your way

- Replace your divots

- Repair your pitch marks

- Make sure you rake a bunker after you have played your shot

- Do not drop litter

Junior Do's & Don'ts of Golf

The Do's

Be ready to play when it is your turn.

Wait until the group in front have moved away from the area you are hitting to.

Stand quietly when someone is playing a shot, even if they are on the hole next to you.

Repair divots and pitch marks on the green. It helps to protect the course and makes it easier for the player behind you.

Allow others to play through if you are searching for a lost ball.

Rake the bunker after you play a shot out of it. If there is no rake try and smooth the sand with your club or your feet.

Replace the flag after you have finished a hole.

Always remember to shout 'FORE' if your ball looks as though it could land close to another golfer.

If someone shouts 'FORE' to you, turn away and protect yourself - don't look around to see who it is!

... and the Don'ts

- Do not move ahead of the person playing their shot. This is dangerous and it can also put the player off their shot.

- Do not make unnecessary noise on the golf course.

- Do not walk on the line of anyone's putt.

- Do not take trolleys onto or too near to the green as they can damage the grass. It is also easier for you to leave your trolley just beyond the green on the way to the next tee. It means you can move onto the next hole quickly and you will not delay golfers playing behind you.

- Do not wait around the green to fill in your scorecard and chat. You can fill in your scorecard when you get to the next tee.

Useful Information

The Dean Davis Golf Show
www.golftrickshotshow.com

Golphin for Kids
www.golphinforkids.com

R & A (Golf's Governing Body)
www.randa.org

Junior Golf Foundation
www.juniorgolfpassport.org

English Golf Union
www.englandgolf.org

Irish Golf Union
www.gui.ie

Scottish golf Union
www.scottishgolf.org

Welsh Golf Union
www.golfunionwales.org